I0756016

FINISHING LINE PRESS
www.finishinglinepress.com

Wheels over Potholes

poems by

Jayanthi Rangan

Finishing Line Press
Georgetown, Kentucky

Wheels over Potholes

ISBN 979-8-89990-418-9 First Edition

ACKNOWLEDGMENTS

"Cluster Bombs Have A Quirk" was first published online by *Rattle Poetry.*

Publisher: Leah Huete de Maines
Editor: Christen Kincaid
Cover Art: Biswajit Mishra
Author Photo: Mallika Rangan
Cover Design: Elizabeth Maines McCleavy

Order online: www.finishinglinepress.com
also available on amazon.com

Author inquiries and mail orders:
Finishing Line Press
PO Box 1626
Georgetown, Kentucky 40324
USA

Contents

For my family—The family I was born into and the family I have gathered and chosen.

Relearning to Stand on his own Feet

Virtual trail walking
on a treadmill, fools the mind
into loving a slog
but at the rehab gym
the walking pad
has a mirror at the end
for the brain to capture
the movement image—
to implant a belief
he is on his feet

He is held in a vertical
position like a rag doll
with the fasteners and ties
of controlled settings
to maneuver the steps
a chance at nerve regeneration
to restore the lost walk

Illusions have power
beliefs have life
they dig for faint spinal pulses
and glue them into a rope
but all the kings' men
and the kings' machines
still couldn't help
the atrophy of his leg muscles

Graduation

He packs for eviction from rehab
glasses, phone, discharge papers
because insurance grants just thirty days
After that, you're out

This morning, four people
hovered in his hospital room
a nurse with pills
a nutritionist with menus
a cleaner changing the linens
an aide stocking blue Gatorade

At home, his wife will be all of them—
nurse, cook, shopper, laundry service
and 3 a.m. emergency crew

He feels bile rise in his throat
Graduation—today is the big day
He glances at the Boston Harbor
from his window at Spaulding rehab

Today, it looks

Opaque, uncharted

Deep and dark blue

Vitals Normal

He lay flat on the ICU bed
A folded towel for a pillow
The bed tilted to 140 degrees
To let him dine on mushy potato

Tomato soup or paste-like swipes
Broccoli goo or bacon glop
After each exhausting meal trial
He'd whisper: *please wipe my mouth*

His kids cheered him with chats
His wife fed him memories
The caregiver cleaned and cathetered
With cool antiseptic wipes

He had been here two weeks now
Aides tilted him to ward off sores
Dozens attended to his comfort
But he just wanted to move—
On his own, turn intentionally

His shrunken sky was white-washed walls
He groaned at the ceiling
Longing to see Sunday night football
Flickering across its blank surface

Ski Moguls

Moguls catch you by surprise—
Before your first chilly inhale is done
Those igloo-looking mounds
Set up their bumpy ambush
Icy, slippery inclines
Where falling flat is the only brake
No wonder it takes Olympian skill
To stay upright in this circus dare

Urinary tract infections
In spinal cord injury patients—
Like moguls, they hit without warning
Dropping amateurs
Onto expert terrain
Without time on the bunny slopes

Before you know what hit you
Bacterial armies reign like oligarchs
Antibiotics become a staple
Doctors scratch their heads
Upping doses and potency of meds
Chasing cures through
Experimental snowdrifts

The ski mounds and bacterial regimes
Bully and procreate with glee

Quiz

What sports can a person play
While in a wheelchair?
He buzzes in the answer
Basketball
Acing the quiz that highlights
Possibilities after spinal cord injury

But this new patient has lost
His mobility, core, and balance—
Lifestyle, hope, and even the basics
Heck, he can barely cough

He looks into his crystal ball
Thrombosis, lung infections
Urinary tract woes
Pain meds, and a burdened life

Will he ever play a game again
His mind frames a blank poster
Words slowly filling in

Life's quiz has no buzzer-beater answers—
Only dribbles
Passes
And rebounds

Freak Accidents

One moment he was whole—
The next, a paraplegic
Tickle and touch: inert on his legs
His bowels stalled
His independence in a coma

Fear stood on both sides
Of the bulletproof glass—
Inside: a man shattered
Outside: lives in smithereens

His legs had been marathoners
They'd stood firm through storms
Pedaled, swum, and sprinted
Now, he longed for a stem to stand on

In the ICU, he stretched his arms—
Gathered his family in a ham-fisted swoop
Through the brace, the tubes, the pain
He whispered: *At least I can still hug you*

A hatchling fell from the family tree.
The mother bird, helpless to rehab
Let the chick lie—
Broken, paralyzed, or maybe dead—
Then flew off to feed the others

No gifts, Please

> *"The meaning of life is to find your gift. The purpose of life is to give it away."*
> *Pablo Picasso*

We played *Clue* and watched *Friends* on TV
Kept holidays calm and always gift-free
It should have been a dream life—but it wasn't
I had spats with my daughter, often

She was a millennial: all strength and form
Who bullied me into the gym—and a membership
Said I was getting older, more likely to fall
I fought her in the car, argued non-stop

But she never wavered on workout time
Held me captive with banter, humor, and madness

Three years later, I weigh the same—
But I've gained balance, core
And what is known as "deceptive strength"

We still don't fall for the glut of gifts
But I cherish the unwrapped present
She forced on me

Haiku

Boston roads in winter
Dent filled—
My arthritic bone

Sole-mate socks—
parted ways
in the washer currents

A.I. couldn't see—
the inner toxic writhing
of a smiling face

Myopia grows
screens babysit all the time—
a blurry vision

Micro-plastic deposits
in lungs—
in war with fresh air

Makeshift Homes

The hermit crab squats
rent-free in a borrowed shell
upgrades to a beachside steal—
just enough room
for creaky joints to dance
with the sea foam

A homeless man scans
for shadows in the city—
unlit storefronts
a junkyard car
turned Buckingham Palace
no guards, no rules

Spinal cord patients
live first in ICU silence
then in the rehab hum—
nurses, therapists
roommates with stories
stitched into the walls

And soldiers
some come back with ghosts
Others, zipped in black
finally find rest
beneath flags
and a polished stone.

Marital Costume

The newborn arrived
coated in goo—
slippery with skin cells
and curdled milk bumps

The father
in his ill-fitting dad-costume
pinched his nostrils—
eew—
a gag caught in his throat

The mother stroked
the freshly cleaned baby
nestled warm
between her breasts
Oooh, she gurgled
My precious

The father
dug for his buried smile
from some deep, dark abyss
and added
She's... cute

New beginnings
new ends—
coated and lumpy
connections

No through-fare

I cannot read his cryptic nerve map—
nor can the doctors
The interpretation key is missing
blocked signals, confusing detours

Figuring out which nerve remains intact
tracing its pathway
is a painstaking trial

Then, his big toe spasms—
jerky and sudden—
the whole foot follows
I film it on my phone
fix it in pixels

He had no sensation—
but now, movement
My hope inflates
like a helium balloon
squeaky with anticipation

The shakes continue
I capture this fuzzy body logo

The doctor sees my filming and says
This means absolutely nothing

Splintering

On the sixth floor of Spaulding Rehab
people with broken spinal cords
describe themselves—
T-5 complete
L4 incomplete—
naming the level of loss

The spine's big bang—
fragmented consciousness
struggling to unite
to become
a whole
a single entity

Stars flung off in tangents
dark matter swirling all around—
planets, comets, meteors
vying to find
their lost alignment

Still Life

The sketch shows a Para-Olympian—
ready for takeoff on his blades
the air around him charged
anticipating lightning

My husband, in his wheelchair
spots the picture and says:
It's a still life—a divot, scooped out
All he is, is an outline
a hollow shell

But I see the flared biceps
the taut abdominals—
one of those paintings
that shifts
with the light
changing shape
with every angle

He Thought of Himself as a Burden

He cried over survival—
why, oh why
His body's machinery splintered
pills a fistful—morning, noon, and night

Living meant hospital visits
pain wrapping around the present

It was a hard path
to make him re-desire the day-to-day
to cherish naps, stretches and showers

Life puzzled him when he stood still
but with that first move
his parachute opened
demystifying this new reality

The cicada resurfaced
from dark depths to light

A Möbius circle—
sometimes inside out
sometimes outside in

The Lines are Down

His legs, clad in khaki shorts and black socks, look normal on the stretcher—yet they jerk in spasms that betray the nerve's silence. He sees the twitching too but feels nothing from the waist down. In the hospital room, his restless legs kick the cellphone off the bed. Onlookers exchange puzzled glances—how can seizures not be *sensation*?

Spastic nerves scream an SOS, a desperate signal trapped in ghost limbs, their message pruned before reaching the brain. The syntax floats without a story—disconnected fragments.

The spasms twist like violent winds swirling around the calm eye of a hurricane—two separate worlds sewn together. The dividing line is faith: faith in neurogenesis.

The brain and nerves will network again, listening, relearning. Some patients regain sensations decades later—those, once unable even to wave, now hold hands. Severed nerves whisper when they're ready.

kintsugi, the showy art of joinery, snuggles breaks.

You Cannot Pour From an Empty Cup

People with broken spines often crave death.
When he fell off his horse and broke his neck
even Superman yearned for it
The guy shot in the back begged for it
The girl who hit the ground running—
now grounded for good—longed for it too

The goodies are gone
What's left is an empty cup
and no one can pour from a void

But at rehab, the volunteers arrive
with stories stitched from scars
their own, or their loved ones'
They come not to fix
but to share their scabs
the bleeds beneath their healing

Somehow, they pour
from what looks like
an empty cup

Diana pulls up in her hand-controlled van
Paul shows off his side-zipped, adaptive pants
It's a relay race, Steve says
Each leg a battle
each victory a baton to pass

Re-walkers move again—
differently
with intention
with a twist

Yes, the cup looks empty
But still—
they pour

Hydrate

My third-grade teacher's mantra was: *Hydrate*
Kids with stomachaches, dizzy spells, or behavior problems
were sent to the water fountain

I thought it worked because it distracted—
took the problem out of the classroom
Turns out my reasoning
was running dry

Later, in a support group
they recommended water to prevent UTIs—
frequent flushes carry the bacteria away
The hemorrhoid doc praised water too

A glut of ailments eased
with plain H_2O
Not just one glass—
but a steady, flowing habit
Healthy change trickles in
over time

Water is subtle, quiet
It works overtime
Unlike medicine
That zaps a fever fast
But rarely stays for the long haul

In third grade, my word was hydrate
Now, as an adult
I've added two more:

Hydrate. Hydrate. Hydrate

A Chat

Scientists want to chat with humpbacks.
"Can we have a playdate?" they ask.
"Any messages for Congress?"

Out of touch with their evolutionary cousins,
armed with only one known word of Whaleen—
a low, throaty twirl of whoop: *hello.*

They start with greetings
end with greetings
Howdy in the middle, howdy in the middle.
Hello... hello, hello... hello, hello... hello...
How many ways can I say hello?

Tongue-tied in Arctic ice
the whales try interpreting human chatter—
no complete sentences, no syntax
just grins and dumbstruck gurgles

Conveying the babble of confused
human nerves and brains is tough
a constriction band, a shifting pain
too much for spinal cords to know

He tries English synonyms
acts it out, touches the sites
points to sensation zones

Neurologists begin to decipher
this living Rosetta Stone.

Earthquakes and Shakes

It started deep beneath the ground
but life trembled at the epicenter
miles away from the break

His T7 vertebra was fractured
though the damage began at T5
Unfelt spasms rippled outward
like the silent shudder of S-waves

Fissures formed in both worlds
the changes, irreversible
One shook the land
the other, his life

The quake's aftershocks were gentler
than the spine's tectonic shifts

Earthquakes have buried faults
Like the tree branch that broke his spine
Too fragile, struck too suddenly
Stresses built—
Seismic.

Cluster bombs have a quirk—

The bomblets don't explode
All at once   but lurk
And layer Cyanide on grief

First   my 1996 Hyundai was snagged
Then my routine tension set in—
Of stretching the dollar like a snake's jaw
Till the next pay check
My six-year-old hiccupped his snotty life
Through his heaving T-shirt
His best friend had found a new best friend

At Lexington Center I waited for the walk sign
When the light blinked   I did too
Rooted   I heard the traffic roar
And the water table of my eyes
Vaguely saw a stranger
Who walked past and then came back—
"May I give you a hug?"
I nodded and he gave—

A tourniquet for my disturbed mind
An eye for the walk-sign

Mood Reset

His accident meddled with living itself
turned our care into something solemn
a heaviness that clung like London fog

Seven months in
he mimicked my nerves
a flicker of somber imitation

We laughed
Our lungs burst with the pain of breath
The pressure cracked—gone, *poof*
The plaque of stress, dissolved

Still lying beneath
the same old sheet of despair
we felt whole again

Decibels We Hear

In the air:
Mute phones gyrating
A greenhouse gas rally
A pollen booth

In water:
A moaning spawn
A town meeting of algae
Aging sediment

On a mountain top:
Pushing ahead
Acing it
An ultraviolet quiet

A Casual Drift

Our home once echoed with laughter inside brick walls—
now doubts and spats stretch us, wall to pick-wall

My husband turns his back; a heaviness fills my chest
Every silence reads like writing on the thick wall

We still agree on how we got to this point
buried beneath the load of a weight-bearing trick wall

We built it ourselves, stone by stony defense
an impenetrable shell, an iron-slick wall

I mourn the loss of sharing, of simple respect
now a gulf, stage-lit by the proscenium flick wall

If only we had listened, not just heard
we might have cracked Berlin's cold, sick wall

Jaya, I whisper through cracks we once ignored—
a name that still echoes off our split wall

Layered Shadow-Box

a young artist glued odd shreds from memory into her shadow box
two baseball ticket stubs, her boyfriend's lone brown sock
a photo of them together, and an empty Starbucks cup

each object, sub-stacked like sediment in a diorama
told the story of her move across states to follow him
his vanishing, her isolation
her trust hardened like crusted paint
her pride too rigid to let her return home

she was done with his betrayal
she was more of a person now
homeless, yes. Boyfriend-less, sure
but intact

she grinned a bitter grin

her art was still hers
her first barista job secure
his face—obscured in the depth
of a two-inch frame

she grinned again
this time a grin of triumph

he was the background in the box
she was inching toward clarity

quaking Aspen –
a leafy moan
a jubilant quiver

Rip Tide

Shallow water climbs to my shoulders
My toes lose grip on the sand—
No anchor now, just drift and dread

I am disoriented
Like a driver without GPS
There are no road signs to guide
Panic swells
I hear an echo: *be calm, be calm*

No lifeguard—not even a straw to grasp
Life drifts away—and I should be calm?
This is a rip tide, and I'm caught in it
Off deserted Playa de Mujeres, San Juan

A puppet, pulled in all directions
Tugged by watery strings
They say: *swim parallel to the shore*
I try

But the rip is strong
It drags me like a net
My qualm: I cannot call to friends
On the shore—my voice won't carry

One thought repeats in my mind
I must remember:

I can swim past this current
Rips are narrow, not very long
But life can

My life can
My life will

Artichokes

The stuffed vegetable looked divine
each leaf slicked with oil
dusted in garlic, parmesan, thyme

I took a hundred photos
dragged the plate closer
unaware of the ritual

Pluck a petal
pinch with teeth
scrape, discard
a rhythm like prayer
or a lab dissection

The pile grew
spent leaves stacked
like mussel shells at low tide

At the core, I met
the fibrous truth
a thistle dressed for dinner

I chewed the cud
of an unbloomed flower
and called it a meal

It wasn't a delicacy
It was a hearty choke

She Practiced Talking Back to her Reflection

She yielded, not voicing her personal boundary
Let others redraw her frontier boundary

She typed each word of growing resolve
Summoning courage to forge a sterner boundary

She longed to belong—but something itched
Their careless laughter chipped at her boundary

Before the mirror, she drilled her lines
"No" isn't cruel—it's just a clearer boundary

Like rivers carve and mountains rise
She learned to honor her nature's boundary

Clarity unlatched her voice, slow but sure
A smile replaced each shrinking boundary

She was claiming space, reshaping the air
Confidence blooming at her firmer boundary

Junction

The body junction was a band
where buzz met numbness
a 3- to 4-inch hell-strip
Magnesium fire sparking nerves
white flare tightening
like a constricting belt
squeezing out air of his lungs

Just like the sky jump—
11,000 feet above ground
trees and power lines
waiting to catch the body

This was the crossing point
between dread and hope
the adrift body
whose future is a blind dive
no promise ahead
and nothing left behind

Hoyer Lift

A Hoyer lift
is a modern-day stork—
not cradling newborns
but raising full-grown men
with machinery

It swings from the hospital ceiling
electrically powered
steady as breath
Today, it carries
a former football player
from bed
to shower

Harnessed at chest and hips
he rises—
weightless for a moment
then lowered again
parking in a tight spot

How I wish I were a Hoyer
for my husband—
not to deliver life
but to lift it higher
to become some super bird
capable of carrying pain away

A Wheelchair is Fully Detachable

It's a thoughtful design—
removable anti-tippers
detachable wheels
a clip-on backrest—
built to fold neatly
into the trunk of a sedan

So many attachable necessities
I secured each notch, each lock
but forget the anti-tippers

As he turned
the chair tipped with a thud—
his crown, his spine
met the unforgiving gym floor

He was too stunned to cry
But my sobs echoed
off polished walls

Caregiving leaves memories—
and bellowing scars
no parts can detach

Teaching Conflict Resolution to a 5-year-old

The breaking news at Kindergarten
was a tiff on the playground—
a shove, a pout, a tiny injustice

Like yeast in a warm bowl
it rose fast
tripled in size over the weekend

The victim's mom heard the story on Friday
By Saturday, she was coaching payback
Next time, don't take it—
hit back harder
They practiced the moves
like dance steps
again and again

Come Monday, before the bell
he found the Friday hitter—
and walloped him to the ground

The teacher had seen
scrapes and skirmishes—
normal storms of small children
but this?
This was warfare
flamed and kneaded by adult hands

Because when you stir the yeast
it stops being flour and water
a new reaction begins—
molecules shift
and heat moves in

Messy Help

> *"Strong women aren't born, they're forged in the fires they've had to walk through."*
> *By Silver Ravenwolf*

The Uber driver left his door ajar
rushed toward my husband
in the wheelchair

I stopped him mid-stride
Please don't help
I'm trained in transferring him

He looked at my small frame
hesitated—then ignored my words

He tangled my husband's legs
unaware of his condition
Fumbling, he muttered:
I can't not help you.

Strength in women
is the far side of the moon—
locked by gravity
seen only from one side

Skill, invisible
until it's interrupted

Across and Down

Two foreigners approached us
in the hotel lobby
they were relaxed businessmen
in dark suits

We stood there in our uniforms—
stewardesses during layover
We judged them by their covers—
so did they

They extended their hands
We didn't shake
We offered Namaste
palms together
which they didn't take

We were a crossword puzzle—
black and white squares
side by side
divided by rules
across and down
each box waiting for
the right clue in the assigned spot

You are not Fat

In fourth grade
he was a packet of yeast—
always rising
the active ingredient in every game
a moving target
no one could quite catch

Still, he said he felt fat
He wanted to work on it
Tell me something I can do about it

I told him
You're fit
You're growing
You're energetic, healthy

But he pressed
No, really
Tell me something I can do

I spoke of metabolism
Of growth spurts
Of how bodies change

He cut through it all
Please
Tell me something I can do

So I told him
about sugar and starch
about labels and hidden syrups
about meals and drinks
and choices

He laughed
He grinned: *I said,*
Tell me something
I can do about it

The Word That Cuts Through the Static

The pyramids in this Mexico City look heavenward—tall in the distance and unreachably steep, its igneous stairs scream to be careful for this is a dizzying experience. Millennia have smoothed them, yet their sharp edges could pitch fork anyone who falls on them.

I collect my water bottle and cap and am all set for the climb. My mother talks to the other tourists and asks for the number of steps to the highest point. She touches her calf and asks for the highlights at the topmost area. She eyes the people sitting and resting on the steps. She is in two minds.

Teotihuacan Gods are afar

I start without her—there are instructions from me to her and her to me. *I will get the best pictures for you but don't forget to wave to me when I call you.* My camera shots are my memory makers so, I click at every light and angle. First base, second base—I try to see this tourist attraction from my mother's point of view—what might interest her fancy?

Mom is way below

Finally, at the top, I focus the camera on my mom, yellow scarf, straw hat and dark glasses. I spot her sitting on the bench but she is looking elsewhere. Will my voice carry across this open space? To get her attention, I call her by her first name, Malathi,—it is an unusual name here. She does not hear me. I fill up my lungs again and scream: once, twice… Heck, I had given her instructions! This is strange, a targeted name yet no results. Many people from the group are looking at me. I yell: "Mom." She hears me instantly, the generic *mom* call alerts her and she smiles for me and raises her hand to wave.

At touching distance, the Hallmark card word.

Girls will be girls?

Once during our family walk—
On the narrow sidewalk up Elm Street
Wild thistles had outgrown the path
The family broke up into two
To get through the narrow sidewalk
The dad and son ahead, mom plus
The daughter a block behind
A limo on the road ahead
Abruptly slowed and stopped
The door swung open but no one
Disembarked or got in
The dad-son duo walked past the revving
As a normal act on road
The women detoured fast
Instinctively away
From open black door
Aware. Knowing.
The game.

A Word of Gratitude

I embraced the grim reality of my husband being in a wheelchair. I was determined to get him through the rough times. However, I couldn't accept the baggage that this spinal cord injury came with—surgeries, spasms, chronic pains, breathing problems, swinging blood pressure, losing voice, weakened hearing, a ruined core and balance, UTI's and so much more.

It was hard to believe that one moment he was a healthy, active professor and the next moment a paraplegic when a tree branch fell on him and altered our lives forever.

This book of poems is my journey through the tunnel where all I heard was static and a wrecking ball, close by. No matter what I saw during that time, it reminded me of the spinal cord injuries and its horrendous impact. If I saw a hilarious video on communications between humans and whales, I immediately thought of the nerve speak between the brain and neurons of spinal cord injury patients. Writing poems was the only thing that helped me stay connected with life during this tough period. *Wheels over Potholes* is a movement of wheelchairs, incidents of hope and inspiration in dark places, stories of courage and persistence and poems that helped me walk the scree slope.

I have included one piece called "Cluster Bombs have a Quirk" that has been curated by Rattle.com. The link is here: https://www.youtube.com/watch?v=G2ens8KPJNs&t=474s

I am thankful for my husband who put in his utmost to be in a better place today, my children, Vikram and Mallika, who immersed their efforts to bring him joy and emotionally enrich his life. Amma, Bala-Kiran, Gopal-Priya and Prabha-Sridhar for being so generous with their time and resources. The younger generation Adit-Jayodita, Sheila, Varun who chose to spend their time with us and the generation alpha who brought in their game of Santa and the Chimney to play with us. My family Sukanya, Hema, Ranjini, Suchi and Mandar, Suren-Mala, Sabitha-Sampath for getting me through tough days, Rev-Ram-Krishna-Kate, Aruna & Jay, Sunitha and Das, Mala-Amitabh/Rita-Sushil, Tara Menon, Mini Jaikumar, Leo Tucker, Fareena Sultan and Laura Moon, forever grateful to all of you.

I cannot comprehend how we could have achieved the stability without the well wishes of the friends and colleagues of my husband. So much to be grateful for. This continued support in this life-long journey, fills me with deep gratitude and strength.

Jayanthi writes poem to renew her lease of life. Her training is in science and her joy and meaning in arts.

Her recent publications are with *Red Noise Collective, Rattle, Hindsight journal, Io Literary journal, Zoetic Press, Stonecrop, Rubbertop, Eclectica, Elevation Review, Rigorous, Poet's Choice, Wingless Dreamer* and *Indolent Books.*

Her short stories are published in *Twisted Vine Literary Publication, Corner Club Press* and *Bookend Review.*

www.ingramcontent.com/pod-product-compliance
Lightning Source LLC
LaVergne TN
LVHW090538110826
845146LV00003B/1168

* 9 7 9 8 8 9 9 9 0 4 1 8 9 *